# S
# TRAVEL GUIDE
# 2023

## *A Trip Preparation Guide to a Romantic Getaway*

## BY

### *Phoenix Cruz*

# TABLE OF CONTENTS

• Budget-friendly options
• Tips for choosing the perfect accommodation

## CHAPTER 4: Sardinia's Best Romantic Experiences
• Discovering Sardinia's hidden beaches
• Taking a romantic sunset hike
• Sampling Sardinian cuisine
• Exploring Sardinia's ancient history and culture
• Relaxing at a spa
• Attending a traditional festival
• Tips for creating your own romantic experiences

## CHAPTER 5: Essential Sardinian Travel Information
• Sardinia's weather and climate
• Health and safety information
• Cultural customs and etiquette
• Useful phrases in Sardinian
• Money-saving tips for your trip

## CONCLUSION
• Final tips for a memorable romantic getaway to Sardinia
• Resources for further travel planning

# INTRODUCTION

Welcome to Sardinia! Located in the Mediterranean Sea, Sardinia is the second-largest island in the Mediterranean and is known for its stunning beaches, crystal-clear waters, rugged mountains, and unique culture. Whether you're looking for a romantic getaway or an adventure-filled vacation, Sardinia has something to offer everyone.

## *Why Sardinia is the Perfect Romantic Getaway*

Sardinia is a great destination for couples looking for a romantic getaway. With its idyllic beaches, warm weather, and charming villages, Sardinia offers the perfect setting for a romantic escape. Couples can explore the island's stunning landscapes, take romantic walks along the beach, dine at intimate restaurants, and indulge in the local wine and cuisine.

In addition to its natural beauty, Sardinia has a rich history and culture. The island is home to ancient ruins, traditional festivals, and unique customs that offer an opportunity for couples to learn about the island's heritage and traditions. The island's luxurious resorts and hotels also provide couples with a romantic and relaxing atmosphere to enjoy each other's company.

## How to Use This Travel Guide

This travel guide is designed to help you plan your trip to Sardinia, whether you're looking for a romantic getaway or an adventure-filled vacation. The guide is divided into several chapters that cover different aspects of your trip, including planning your trip, choosing your itinerary, where to stay, and essential travel information.

Each chapter provides comprehensive information and useful tips to help you make the most of your trip.

# CHAPTER 1

## Planning Your Trip to Sardinia

Sardinia is a hidden gem in the Mediterranean, with its beautiful beaches, turquoise waters, and rugged mountains. However, planning a trip to this unique destination can be overwhelming, especially if you're not familiar with the island.

In this chapter, we'll cover everything you need to know to plan your Sardinian adventure, including the best time to go, how to get there, getting around the island, and travel tips for a hassle-free trip.

I'll also provide you with important information about Sardinia's visa requirements, so you can ensure that you have all the necessary documentation before you leave.

Whether you're a first-time traveler or a seasoned adventurer, this chapter will help you plan a stress-free and unforgettable trip to Sardinia. So let's dive in and start planning your dream getaway to this stunning island!

## When To Go

Choosing the right time to visit Sardinia is important to make the most out of your trip. Sardinia has a Mediterranean climate, with mild winters and hot summers. The island enjoys a long tourist season that runs from April to October, with peak season from July to August.

✓ Summer (June to September) is the most popular time to visit Sardinia due to its warm and sunny weather. However, this also means that the beaches and tourist destinations can be crowded, and accommodation prices can be high. If you're planning to visit during the summer months, it's recommended to book your accommodation and activities well in advance.

✓ Spring (April to May) and autumn (October to November) are also great times to visit Sardinia, with fewer tourists and more pleasant temperatures. The landscapes are at their most beautiful during these seasons, with wildflowers blooming in spring and autumnal foliage in fall.

✓ Winter (December to March) is the off-season in Sardinia, with cooler temperatures and occasional rainfall. However, this is a great time to visit if you're looking for a quieter and more budget-friendly trip. Many restaurants and attractions are closed during this season, so it's important to plan ahead and check the opening times before you go.

Overall, the best time to visit Sardinia depends on your preferences and what you want to do. If you're looking for a lively atmosphere and want to enjoy the beaches, then summer is the best time to go. If you prefer a quieter trip and want to explore the island's nature and history, then spring and autumn are ideal. And if you're on a budget, then winter is the best season to find great deals on accommodation and activities.

Whatever time of the year you choose to go, Sardinia will offer you stunning landscapes, crystal-clear waters, and unique cultural experiences that will leave you with unforgettable memories.

## *How To Get There*

Sardinia is an island located in the Mediterranean Sea, and there are several ways to get there depending on your location and preferences.

**1. By Air:** The easiest way to reach Sardinia is by air, and the island has three international airports: Cagliari-Elmas, Olbia-Costa Smeralda, and Alghero-Fertilia. These airports receive regular flights from major European cities such as London, Paris, Rome, and Madrid, as well as domestic flights from Italian cities.

**2. By Sea:** If you're coming from mainland Italy, you can also reach Sardinia by ferry. The island has several ports that offer regular ferry services, such as Porto Torres, Olbia, Cagliari, and Arbatax. The ferry services operate from various Italian cities such as Rome, Genoa, and Livorno.

**3. By Train and Bus:** Another option to reach Sardinia is by train and bus. However, this can be a longer and more complicated journey, as there are no direct train or bus connections from the Italian mainland to Sardinia. You'll need to take a train or bus to one of the ports, such as Genoa or Livorno, and then take a ferry to the island.

**4. Getting Around the Island:** Once you're on the island, the best way to get around is by car. Sardinia has an extensive road network, and car rental services are available at the airports and ports. However, it's important to note that driving in Sardinia can be challenging due to narrow roads, winding mountain passes, and occasional traffic.

**5. Public transportation** is also available, with buses connecting major towns and cities. However, the services can be infrequent, especially in rural areas, and may not operate on Sundays and public holidays.

# Getting Around Sardinia

Sardinia is a beautiful island with a diverse range of landscapes, from sandy beaches to rugged mountains, making it an ideal place for exploring.
Here are some of the ways you can get around the island:

**1. Car Rental:** Renting a car is the most convenient way to get around Sardinia. All major car rental companies have branches at the airports, and you can also rent a car at the ports. Having a car will give you the flexibility to explore the island at your own pace and discover hidden gems that may not be accessible by public transportation. However, it's important to note that driving in Sardinia can be challenging due to narrow and winding roads, especially in mountainous areas.

**2. Public Transportation:** Sardinia has a network of buses that connect major towns and cities. ARST is the main bus company on the island, and you can buy tickets at the bus stations, bars, and tobacco shops. The buses are generally clean and comfortable, but the services can be infrequent, especially in rural areas, and may not operate on Sundays and public holidays. It's recommended to check the bus schedules and plan your itinerary accordingly.

**3. Trains:** Sardinia has a limited train service, with only a few lines connecting major towns and cities. The trains are operated by Trenitalia, and you can buy tickets at the train stations or online. However, the trains are generally slower than buses, and the services can be infrequent, so it's important to plan your itinerary accordingly.

**4. Taxi:** Taxis are available in Sardinia, and you can either hail one on the street or book one in advance. However, taxis can be expensive, especially for long journeys, and may not be a feasible option for budget travelers.

**5. Bicycle:** Bicycling is another way to explore Sardinia, and there are several bike rental shops on the island. Cycling is a great way to discover the island's natural beauty, and there are many bike-friendly routes, such as the La Maddalena Archipelago and Costa Smeralda.

# Travel Tips For A Hassle-free Trip

Planning a trip to Sardinia can be exciting, but it's important to take some precautions to ensure a hassle-free journey. Here are some travel tips to help you have a smooth trip:

**1. Check Your Passport and Visa Requirements:** Before traveling to Sardinia, make sure to check your passport and visa requirements. Citizens of the European Union, Switzerland, Norway, Iceland, and Liechtenstein do not need a visa to enter Sardinia. However, travelers from other countries should check with the Italian embassy or consulate to ensure they have the necessary documents for entry.

**2. Book Accommodations in Advance:** Sardinia is a popular tourist destination, and accommodations can fill up quickly, especially during peak season. It's recommended to book your accommodations in advance to avoid any last-minute hassle. There are plenty of options for every budget, including hotels, bed and breakfasts, and vacation rentals.

**3. Pack for the Weather:** Sardinia has a Mediterranean climate, with mild winters and hot summers. It's important to pack appropriate clothing for the weather, especially if you plan on exploring the outdoors. Bring light and breathable clothing for the summer months, and a jacket or sweater for cooler evenings. Also, don't forget to pack sunscreen, sunglasses, and a hat to protect yourself from the sun.

**4. Learn Basic Italian:** Italian is the official language of Sardinia, and while many locals speak English, it's helpful to learn some basic Italian phrases. This can help you communicate with locals and make your trip more enjoyable.

**5. Be Mindful of Local Customs:** Sardinia has a rich cultural heritage, and it's important to be respectful of local customs and traditions. Dress modestly when visiting religious sites, and avoid taking photos of people without their permission. Also, be mindful of meal times, as many restaurants close during the afternoon and reopen in the evening.

**6. Take Care of Your Valuables:** Sardinia is a safe destination, but it's always important to take care of your valuables. Keep your money, passport, and other important documents in a safe place, and avoid carrying large amounts of cash. Also, be cautious when using ATMs and credit cards, and notify your bank of your travel plans in advance.

Overall, with proper planning and precautions, you can have a wonderful and memorable experience on this beautiful island.

## Sardinia's Visa Requirements

Sardinia is a region in Italy, and as such, the visa requirements for Sardinia are the same as those for Italy.

Citizens of the European Union, Switzerland, Norway, Iceland, and Liechtenstein do not need a visa to enter Sardinia, as they have the right to free movement within the European Union. They only need to present a valid passport or national ID card to enter the country.

Citizens of many other countries, including the United States, Canada, Australia, and Japan, do not need a visa for stays of up to 90 days for tourism or business purposes. However, they do need a valid passport that is not set to expire within six months of their arrival date, and they may be asked to show proof of return or onward travel.

Citizens of some countries, such as China, Russia, India, and Nigeria, need a Schengen visa to enter Sardinia. The Schengen visa is a short-stay visa that allows travelers to stay in the Schengen Area, which includes Italy, for up to 90 days within a six-month period. To obtain a Schengen visa, travelers must apply at the embassy or consulate of the country where they will spend the most time during their trip, or the country where they will first enter the Schengen Area.

To apply for a Schengen visa, travelers must provide several documents, including a passport with at least two blank pages, a completed visa application form, a recent passport-sized photo, proof of travel insurance, proof of accommodation and flight reservations, and proof of financial means to cover their stay in the Schengen Area.

It's important to note that visa requirements and regulations can change, so travelers should always check with the Italian embassy or consulate in their country before planning their trip to Sardinia. They should also allow plenty of time to apply for a visa if necessary, as the process can take several weeks or even months.

# CHAPTER 2

## Choosing Your Sardinia Itinerary

As you plan your dream trip to Sardinia, you'll quickly realize that there are countless ways to spend your time in this beautiful region of Italy. From sun-soaked beaches to rugged mountains, ancient ruins to modern art museums, Sardinia offers a wealth of options for every traveler.

But with so many choices, it can be overwhelming to decide how to spend your time in Sardinia. That's where this chapter comes in. Here, I'll guide you through the process of choosing the Sardinia itinerary that's perfect for you.

Whether you're a beach lover, a history buff, a foodie, or an adventure seeker, I'll help you create an itinerary that fits your interests and travel style. I'll highlight the must-see sights in each region of Sardinia, as well as some hidden gems that are off the beaten path.

So sit back, grab a cup of coffee or a glass of wine, and get ready to plan the trip of a lifetime with your loved one (definitely). With this chapter as your guide, you'll be able to create an itinerary that's tailored to your interests and preferences, ensuring that you make the most of your time in beautiful Sardinia.

# Recommended Itineraries For a Romantic Getaway

Sardinia is a popular destination for couples looking for a romantic getaway, with its stunning beaches, charming towns, and beautiful landscapes. If you're planning a romantic trip to Sardinia, here are some recommended itineraries that will help you make the most of your time in this beautiful region of Italy:

**1. The Costa Smeralda Itinerary:** The Costa Smeralda is one of the most famous and luxurious destinations in Sardinia, known for its beautiful beaches and glamorous resorts. Start your trip in Porto Cervo, the heart of the Costa Smeralda, and spend your days lounging on the beach, shopping in designer boutiques, and dining in gourmet restaurants. You can also take a boat tour to the nearby islands of La Maddalena and Caprera, or explore the nearby town of Olbia.

**2. The Alghero and Bosa Itinerary:** Alghero is a charming town on the northwest coast of Sardinia, known for its beautiful historic center and stunning beaches. Spend a few days exploring the town's narrow streets and ancient walls, and then head south to the town of Bosa, known for its colorful houses and picturesque river. You can also take a day trip to the nearby Grotte di Nettuno, a stunning network of caves and underground lakes.

**3. The Ogliastra Itinerary:** Ogliastra is a less-touristy region of Sardinia, known for its rugged mountains, pristine beaches, and traditional villages. Start your trip in the town of Tortolì, and spend your days hiking in the mountains, swimming in the sea, and exploring the region's many ancient ruins. You can also take a day trip to the nearby town of Baunei, known for its stunning views over the coast.

**4. The Southern Sardinia Itinerary:** The southern part of Sardinia is known for its stunning beaches and crystal-clear waters. Start your trip in the town of Cagliari, the capital of Sardinia, and spend your days exploring the town's historic center, lounging on the nearby beaches, and visiting nearby sights such as the ancient ruins of Nora and the flamingo-filled lagoon of Santa Gilla.

**5. The Nuoro and Barbagia Itinerary:** Nuoro is the cultural heart of Sardinia, known for its traditional festivals, historic museums, and beautiful mountains. Start your trip in Nuoro, and spend your days exploring the town's many museums, visiting traditional villages in the nearby Barbagia region, and hiking in the nearby mountains. You can also take a day trip to the stunning Cala Gonone, known for its beautiful beaches and crystal-clear waters.

**6. The Oristano and Sinis Peninsula Itinerary:** Oristano is a charming town on the west coast of Sardinia, known for its medieval center and traditional festivals. Spend a few days exploring the town's many historic sites, and then head to the nearby Sinis Peninsula, known for its stunning beaches and ancient ruins. You can also take a day trip to the nearby town of Bosa, known for its colorful houses and picturesque river.

**7. The Maddalena Archipelago Itinerary:** The Maddalena Archipelago is a group of islands off the coast of Sardinia, known for their crystal-clear waters and stunning beaches. Start your trip in the town of Palau, and take a ferry to the main island of La Maddalena. Spend your days exploring the island's many beaches and hiking trails, and take a boat tour to nearby islands such as Caprera and Spargi.

**8. The Castelsardo and Stintino Itinerary:** Castelsardo is a picturesque town on the north coast of Sardinia, known for its medieval castle and stunning views over the sea. Spend a few days exploring the town's historic center, and then head to the nearby town of Stintino, known for its beautiful beaches and crystal-clear waters. You can also take a day trip to the nearby Asinara Island, known for its stunning natural beauty and wildlife.

**9. The San Teodoro and Olbia Itinerary:** San Teodoro is a popular tourist destination on the east coast of Sardinia, known for its beautiful beaches and lively nightlife. Spend a few days lounging on the beach and exploring the town's many shops and restaurants, and then head to the nearby town of Olbia. You can also take a day trip to the nearby Tavolara Island, known for its stunning views and clear waters.

No matter which itinerary you choose, Sardinia is sure to provide the perfect romantic backdrop for your getaway. With its stunning scenery, delicious food, and relaxed atmosphere, it's no wonder that so many couples choose to visit this beautiful region of Italy.

## Creating Your Own Itinerary

While there are many pre-planned itineraries available for a romantic getaway in Sardinia, some travelers prefer to create their own itinerary based on their specific interests and preferences. Here are some tips on creating your own itinerary for a memorable trip to Sardinia:

**1. Research your options:** Start by researching the different towns, attractions, and activities that Sardinia has to offer (That has been covered in this book already).

**2. Consider your interests:** Think about what you and your partner enjoy doing together, whether it's hiking, swimming, shopping, or exploring historic sites. Make a list of the activities and attractions that interest you the most.

**3. Determine your travel style:** Consider whether you prefer a fast-paced trip with lots of activities and sightseeing or a more relaxed trip with plenty of time for lounging on the beach and enjoying each other's company.

**4. Map out your route:** Once you have an idea of what you want to see and do, map out your route. Determine the best way to get from one destination to another, and factor in travel time and distance.

**5. Allow for flexibility:** While it's important to have a plan in place, be sure to allow for flexibility. Leave some room in your itinerary for unexpected detours, weather changes, and other unforeseen events.

**6. Prioritize your must-sees:** If you have limited time, make a list of your must-see attractions and prioritize them. This will ensure that you don't miss out on the experiences that are most important to you.

**7. Get advice from locals:** Don't be afraid to ask for advice from locals, whether it's a hotel concierge, a restaurant owner, or a friendly local you meet on the street. They can provide valuable insights and recommendations.

By following these tips, you can create an itinerary that is tailored to your unique interests and preferences, ensuring a memorable and enjoyable romantic getaway in Sardinia.

# Tips For Getting The Most Out Of Your Trip

When planning a trip to Sardinia for a romantic getaway, there are several tips that can help you get the most out of your experience. Here are some tips to keep in mind:

**1. Slow down:** Sardinia is a beautiful and relaxing destination, so don't try to cram too many activities into your itinerary. Take the time to savor the scenery and enjoy each other's company.

**2. Embrace the culture:** Sardinia has a unique culture that is worth exploring. Sample the local cuisine, visit museums and art galleries, and attend cultural events and festivals.

**3. Go off the beaten path:** While popular tourist destinations can be enjoyable, consider exploring some lesser-known areas to truly experience the island's beauty and charm. Talk to locals and get their recommendations for hidden gems.

**4. Take advantage of outdoor activities:** Sardinia's natural beauty lends itself to outdoor activities like hiking, swimming, and boating. Consider booking a guided excursion or renting equipment to experience the island's natural wonders.

**5. Stay in local accommodations:** Consider staying in a local bed and breakfast or rental property to get a more authentic experience of Sardinian life. This can also provide a more intimate and romantic setting for your trip.

**6. Learn some Italian:** While many locals speak English, learning some basic Italian phrases can help you communicate better and show respect for the local culture.

**7. Pack appropriately:** Sardinia has a Mediterranean climate, so be sure to pack comfortable clothing suitable for warm temperatures. Don't forget to pack sunscreen, hats, and sunglasses to protect against the sun.

By following these tips, you can make the most of your romantic getaway to Sardinia and create memories that will last a lifetime.

# CHAPTER 3

## Where to Stay in Sardinia

Finding the perfect place to stay is an important part of any romantic getaway, and Sardinia offers a variety of options to suit every taste and budget. Whether you prefer a luxury resort, a charming bed and breakfast, or a quaint seaside villa, Sardinia has it all. In this chapter, we'll explore the different areas of Sardinia and provide recommendations for the best places to stay for a romantic getaway. From idyllic beachfront locations to cozy mountain retreats, I'll help you find the perfect accommodation to make your trip to Sardinia unforgettable.

## Overview of Sardinia's accommodations

Sardinia offers a wide variety of accommodations to suit every traveler's needs and budget. From luxurious five-star resorts to cozy bed and breakfasts, there is something for everyone on this beautiful island. Here is an overview of the types of accommodations you can find in Sardinia:

**1. Luxury resorts:** Sardinia is home to several high-end luxury resorts that offer top-notch amenities and services. These resorts are typically located in beautiful beachfront locations and feature luxurious rooms, spas, restaurants, and other upscale amenities.

**2. Boutique hotels:** For travelers who want a more intimate and personalized experience, Sardinia has several boutique hotels to choose from. These smaller hotels offer unique decor, personalized service, and a more intimate atmosphere than larger resorts.

**3. Bed and breakfasts:** Sardinia is home to many charming bed and breakfasts that offer a cozy and welcoming atmosphere. These accommodations are typically run by local families and offer a more authentic experience of Sardinian life.

**4. Vacation rentals:** For travelers who prefer a more independent experience, vacation rentals are a popular option in Sardinia. These can range from apartments and villas to cottages and farmhouses, and provide a great opportunity to live like a local while enjoying the island's natural beauty.

**5. Agriturismo:** Sardinia is famous for its agricultural traditions, and agriturismo accommodations allow travelers to experience these traditions firsthand. These accommodations are typically located on working farms or vineyards and offer an immersive experience of rural life in Sardinia.

No matter what type of accommodation you prefer, Sardinia offers a range of options to suit every taste and budget. By carefully considering your needs and preferences, you can find the perfect place to stay for your romantic getaway to this beautiful island.

# Luxury Resorts And Hotels

Sardinia is home to several luxurious five-star resorts and hotels that offer top-notch amenities and services for a truly indulgent and memorable stay. Here is an overview of some of the best luxury accommodations in Sardinia:

**1. Hotel Cala di Volpe:** Located on the Costa Smeralda, Hotel Cala di Volpe is one of the most iconic luxury hotels in Sardinia. This 5-star hotel features beautifully designed rooms and suites with stunning sea views, a private beach, a spa, and several gourmet restaurants.

**2. Hotel Romazzino:** Another luxury hotel on the Costa Smeralda, Hotel Romazzino boasts a prime location on a private beach with crystal-clear waters. The hotel features beautifully designed rooms and suites with sea views, a spa, a fitness center, and several gourmet restaurants.

**3. Forte Village Resort:** This sprawling resort is located on the southern coast of Sardinia and offers a wide range of luxurious accommodations, including villas, bungalows, and suites. The resort features several private beaches, a spa, a golf course, and a range of activities and entertainment options.

**4. La Villa del Re:** This small luxury hotel is located on a secluded beach in Costa Rei and offers a peaceful and intimate atmosphere for a romantic getaway. The hotel features elegantly designed rooms and suites, a private beach, a spa, and a gourmet restaurant.

**5. Su Gologone Experience Hotel:** This charming hotel is located in the heart of Sardinia's rugged interior and offers a unique and authentic Sardinian experience. The hotel features beautifully decorated rooms and suites, a spa, and several restaurants serving traditional Sardinian cuisine.

These luxury resorts and hotels offer unparalleled comfort and service for an indulgent and unforgettable stay in Sardinia. Whether you're looking for a beachfront escape or a secluded mountain retreat, these accommodations are sure to exceed your expectations.

# Cozy Bed and Breakfasts

If you're looking for a more intimate and affordable option for your stay in Sardinia, then cozy bed and breakfasts may be the perfect choice for you. Here is an overview of some of the best bed and breakfasts in Sardinia:

**1. B&B Antico Borgo:** Located in the charming town of Alghero, B&B Antico Borgo is housed in a beautifully restored 18th-century building. The B&B features comfortable and tastefully decorated rooms, a shared lounge area, and a terrace with stunning views of the town.

**2. B&B Il Giardino Segreto:** This charming bed and breakfast is located in the historic center of Cagliari, Sardinia's capital city. The B&B features elegantly furnished rooms, a peaceful garden, and a delicious breakfast served every morning.

**3. B&B Alghero In:** Another great option in Alghero, B&B Alghero In is located just a short walk from the town's historic center and the beach. The B&B features cozy rooms with private bathrooms, a shared kitchen and dining area, and a lovely terrace.

**4. B&B La Dolce Vita:** This cozy bed and breakfast is located in the picturesque town of Castelsardo on the northern coast of Sardinia. The B&B features comfortable rooms with sea views, a shared lounge area, and a terrace overlooking the sea.

**5. B&B Luce Viola:** This charming bed and breakfast is located in the heart of the medieval town of Bosa on the west coast of Sardinia. The B&B features cozy and stylishly decorated rooms, a shared lounge area, and a lovely terrace with panoramic views of the town and the river.

These cozy bed and breakfasts offer a warm and welcoming atmosphere, personalized service, and a great value for your money. Whether you're looking for a romantic escape or a cultural adventure, these bed and breakfasts are sure to make your stay in Sardinia unforgettable.

# Budget-Friendly Options

If you're on a tight budget but still want to experience the beauty of Sardinia, there are plenty of budget-friendly accommodation options to choose from. Here are some of the best options for travelers looking for affordable lodging:

**1. Hostels:** Sardinia has a great selection of hostels, ranging from basic dorm-style accommodations to private rooms. Hostels are a great option for solo travelers, backpackers, and groups of friends looking for a cheap place to stay. Some of the best hostels in Sardinia include Hostel Marina in Cagliari, Hostel Brikette in Alghero, and Geko Hostel & Pousada in Olbia.

**2. Camping:** If you enjoy the great outdoors, then camping in Sardinia is a great option. The island has plenty of campsites, ranging from basic tent sites to more luxurious options with cabins and bungalows. Some of the best campsites in Sardinia include Is Arenas

Camping Village in Oristano, Tonnara Camping in Stintino, and Camping Capo d'Orso in Palau.

**3. Agriturismi:** Agriturismi are farmhouses that offer accommodation to travelers. They are a great option for those looking for an authentic and affordable experience. Many agriturismi offer meals made from locally sourced ingredients and activities such as horseback riding, hiking, and cooking classes. Some of the best agriturismi in Sardinia include Su Pinnettu in Arbus, Agriturismo Sa Mola in Orosei, and Agriturismo Don Ballore in Bosa.

**4. Vacation rentals:** Another great option for budget-friendly lodging in Sardinia is vacation rentals. These can include apartments, villas, and houses that are rented out by the owner. Vacation rentals offer more space and privacy than a hotel room and can be a great option for families or groups of friends. Some of the best vacation rental options in Sardinia can be found on websites such as Airbnb, HomeAway, and VRBO.

Overall, Sardinia offers plenty of affordable accommodation options for travelers on a budget. Whether you choose to stay in a hostel, campsite, agriturismo, or vacation rental, you're sure to find a comfortable and affordable place to rest your head while exploring the beauty of this stunning island.

# Tips for Choosing the Perfect Accommodation

Choosing the right accommodation is an important part of planning your trip to Sardinia. With so many options available, it can be overwhelming to decide where to stay. Here are some tips to help you choose the perfect accommodation for your trip:

**1. Location:** When choosing accommodation, consider the location. Do you want to be in the heart of the city, near the beach, or in a rural area? Think about what you want to see and do during your trip and choose an accommodation that is conveniently located to those activities.

**2. Budget:** Determine your budget before you start looking for accommodation. This will help you narrow down your options and avoid overspending. Remember to factor in additional costs such as transportation and food when setting your budget.

**3. Amenities:** Consider the amenities that are important to you. Do you want a pool, a gym, or a spa? Do you need a kitchenette or a balcony? Make a list of the amenities that you desire and use that list to narrow down your options.

**4. Reviews:** Before booking any accommodation, be sure to read reviews from previous guests. Look for common themes in the reviews, such as cleanliness, customer service, and location. Reviews can provide valuable insight into what to expect from your stay.

**5. Type of accommodation:** Consider the type of accommodation that best suits your needs. Are you looking for a hotel, a bed and breakfast, or an apartment? Each type of accommodation has its own advantages and disadvantages, so choose the one that best fits your preferences.

**6. Customer service:** When choosing accommodation, pay attention to the customer service. Look for properties with responsive and helpful staff that can assist with any questions or concerns that you may have during your stay.

**7. Safety and security:** Make sure that the accommodation you choose is safe and secure. Look for properties with security features such as locks on doors and windows, smoke detectors, and fire extinguishers.

**8. Accessibility:** If you have any mobility concerns or disabilities, make sure that the accommodation you choose is accessible. Look for properties with features such as wheelchair ramps, grab bars, and elevators.

**9. Special offers and deals:** Keep an eye out for special offers and deals when booking accommodation. Many properties offer discounts for booking in advance, staying for multiple nights, or booking through certain websites.

Overall, choosing the perfect accommodation in Sardinia requires careful consideration of your preferences, needs, and budget. Use these tips to help you narrow down your options and find the perfect place to stay for a comfortable and enjoyable trip.

# CHAPTER 4

## Sardinia's Best Romantic Experiences

In this chapter, we'll be delving into the best romantic experiences that this stunning island has to offer. Sardinia is a place of unparalleled beauty and wonder, where crystal clear waters lap against white sandy beaches, and rugged mountain ranges tower above verdant forests. It's the perfect destination for a romantic getaway, with plenty of opportunities for couples to create unforgettable memories together.

Whether you're looking for a secluded beach to watch the sunset, a hidden cove to explore by boat, or a charming hilltop village to wander hand in hand, Sardinia has something to offer every couple. In this chapter, I'll be sharing my top picks for the most romantic experiences on the island, as well as some insider tips to help you make the most of your time in this magical place. So let's dive in and discover the romantic side of Sardinia!

# Discovering Sardinia's Hidden Beaches

Sardinia is home to some of the most beautiful beaches in the world, with crystal clear waters, white sands, and stunning scenery. While some of the island's beaches are popular tourist destinations, there are also many hidden gems waiting to be discovered by those who are willing to venture off the beaten path. In this section, I'll be sharing some tips for discovering Sardinia's hidden beaches and experiencing their natural beauty.

**1. Explore by boat**
One of the best ways to discover Sardinia's hidden beaches is by boat. Rent a boat or join a guided tour and explore the coastline at your own pace. Many of the island's hidden beaches are only accessible by boat, and you'll be able to see the stunning rock formations and cliffs from a unique perspective.

## 2. Venture off the beaten path

If you're up for a bit of adventure, venture off the beaten path and explore the island's rugged coastline on foot. Many of Sardinia's hidden beaches can only be reached by hiking along narrow trails or scrambling over rocky terrain, but the effort is well worth it for the secluded and untouched beauty that awaits.

## 3. Visit during the off-season

During peak tourist season, many of Sardinia's popular beaches can get crowded and busy. However, if you visit during the off-season, you'll have a better chance of discovering the island's hidden beaches without the crowds. The weather may be cooler, but you'll be rewarded with a more peaceful and intimate experience.

## 4. Respect the environment

When visiting Sardinia's hidden beaches, it's important to respect the environment and leave no trace behind. Take your rubbish with you, avoid disturbing the local wildlife, and follow any rules or regulations that may be in place to protect the area.

# Taking a Romantic Sunset Hike

Sardinia's stunning natural beauty is not only limited to its beaches, but also extends to its rugged hills and mountains. One of the most romantic ways to experience this natural beauty is by taking a sunset hike with your partner. In this section, we'll explore some tips for taking a romantic sunset hike in Sardinia.

**1. Choose the right trail:** When choosing a trail for your sunset hike, it's important to consider the level of difficulty and the time it will take to complete the hike. You don't want to be rushing to finish the hike before the sun sets, or risk getting lost in the dark. Look for a trail that's appropriate for your skill level and that has a clear path to follow.

**2. Plan your timing:** Timing is everything when it comes to taking a romantic sunset hike. Check the sunset time and plan your hike accordingly, allowing plenty of time to reach your destination and set up for the sunset. It's also important to consider the time it will take to hike back to your starting point or to your accommodation after the sun sets.

**3. Bring the right gear:** When hiking in Sardinia, it's important to wear appropriate clothing and footwear, especially if you're hiking in the cooler months. Bring a warm jacket, a hat, and gloves if necessary. Don't forget to bring water and snacks, as well as a flashlight or headlamp in case you get caught out in the dark.

**4. Choose a scenic spot:** To fully enjoy the sunset, it's important to choose a scenic spot with a clear view of the horizon. Look for a viewpoint, hilltop, or other high point that offers an unobstructed view of the sunset. You can also research online or ask locals for recommendations on the best spots for sunset watching.

**5. Enjoy the moment:** Finally, remember to take your time and enjoy the moment with your partner. Savor the natural beauty of Sardinia, watch the sunset, and take in the breathtaking views around you. This is a special moment to be cherished, so don't rush it and allow yourself to fully immerse in the experience.

## Sampling Sardinian Cuisine

Sardinia is a paradise for foodies, offering a unique and diverse culinary tradition that draws inspiration from its history, culture, and natural resources. In this section, we'll explore some tips for sampling Sardinian cuisine and savoring its flavors and aromas.

**1. Discover Sardinian specialties:** Sardinia has a rich culinary heritage that showcases its unique geography and history. From the succulent roasted lamb of the mountainous regions to the fresh seafood of the coast, Sardinian cuisine offers a diverse range of specialties that will tantalize your taste buds. Some of the must-try dishes include culurgiones (a type of ravioli stuffed with potato and mint), porceddu (roasted suckling pig), and seadas (a dessert made with cheese, honey, and lemon zest).

**2. Visit local markets and restaurants:** One of the best ways to sample Sardinian cuisine is to visit local markets and restaurants. Local markets are great places to discover fresh ingredients, including vegetables, fruits, cheese, and meat. You can also find locally produced wine, honey, and olive oil. In restaurants, you can taste traditional Sardinian dishes prepared by skilled chefs and paired with local wines. Look for restaurants that offer a menu featuring local ingredients and dishes.

**3. Try Sardinian wines:** Sardinia is also famous for its wines, which range from crisp whites to full-bodied reds. Some of the most famous Sardinian wines include Cannonau (a red wine made from Grenache grapes), Vermentino (a white wine with a citrusy flavor), and Malvasia (a sweet wine with notes of honey and apricot). You can taste Sardinian wines at local wineries, wine bars, and restaurants.

**4. Attend food festivals and events:** Sardinia is home to numerous food festivals and events throughout the year, celebrating the island's culinary traditions and local specialties. These festivals are great opportunities to taste authentic Sardinian cuisine, listen to traditional music, and participate in local customs and traditions. Some of the most popular food festivals include Sagra del Redentore (a festival dedicated to roasted lamb), Sagra del Mirto (a festival celebrating the myrtle plant), and Autunno in Barbagia (a festival showcasing local food, crafts, and traditions).

**5. Learn to cook Sardinian dishes:** Finally, if you're a food enthusiast, you can learn to cook Sardinian dishes yourself. Many cooking schools and culinary tours offer classes and workshops that teach traditional Sardinian recipes and cooking techniques. You can also visit local farms and cheese factories to learn how Sardinian cheese is made, or participate in wine tastings and tours to learn about Sardinian wine production.

# Exploring Sardinia's Ancient History and Culture

Sardinia is not only famous for its breathtaking beaches and natural beauty but also for its ancient history and culture. The island has a rich and diverse cultural heritage, shaped by its past rulers, including the Phoenicians, Romans, and Spanish.

**1. Visit Nuraghe:** Nuraghe is a type of ancient megalithic structure found only in Sardinia. These cone-shaped towers were built by the Nuragic civilization, which inhabited the island from the Bronze Age until the 2nd century AD. There are over 7,000 Nuraghe structures in Sardinia, and some of the best-preserved ones include Nuraghe Su Nuraxi, Nuraghe Losa, and Nuraghe Santu Antine. Visiting these ancient structures is an excellent way to learn about Sardinia's unique and ancient history.

**2. Explore Museums and Archaeological Sites:** Sardinia is home to many museums and archaeological sites that showcase the island's rich history and culture. The National Archaeological Museum of Cagliari is a must-visit for those interested in Sardinia's past. The museum has a vast collection of artifacts, including Bronze Age and Nuragic pottery, Roman statues, and medieval art. The Tharros Archaeological Site, located on the west coast of Sardinia, is another popular attraction. The site contains ancient ruins, including the remains of a Roman city and a Punic settlement.

**3. Attend Festivals and Events:** Sardinia hosts many festivals and events throughout the year, which provide a unique opportunity to experience the island's culture and traditions. One of the most popular events is the Sagra del Redentore in Nuoro, which takes place every August. This festival features traditional music, dance, and food, and attracts thousands of locals and tourists every year. Another popular event is the Sa Sartiglia in Oristano, a carnival-like festival that includes horse races and traditional costumes.

**4. Visit Ancient Churches and Basilicas**: Sardinia has a rich Christian heritage, and the island is home to many ancient churches and basilicas. The Basilica di San Gavino in Porto Torres is one of the most impressive, with its imposing Romanesque facade and ancient crypt. Another popular church is the Chiesa di Santa Maria del Regno in Ardara, which features a stunning Baroque interior and a beautiful wooden altar.

**5. Enjoy Local Festivities:** One of the best ways to experience Sardinia's culture is by enjoying the local festivities. These events offer a unique opportunity to taste traditional Sardinian cuisine, listen to local music, and experience the island's vibrant atmosphere. Some of the most popular festivities include the Festa di San Simplicio in Olbia, the Festa di Sant'Efisio in Cagliari, and the Festa di Sant'Antonio Abate in Mamoiada.

Overall, Sardinia's ancient history and culture are an essential part of the island's unique identity. Exploring the island's past and traditions is an excellent way to enhance your Sardinian experience and gain a deeper appreciation of the island's beauty and charm.

# Relaxing at a Spa

If you're looking for some relaxation and rejuvenation during your romantic getaway in Sardinia, a visit to one of the island's many spas is a must. Sardinia is home to a number of luxury spa resorts that offer a wide range of treatments, including massages, facials, body scrubs, and hydrotherapy.

Some of the most popular spas in Sardinia are located in the northern part of the island, near the famous Costa Smeralda. One of the most well-known is the Acquaforte Thalasso & Spa, located at the Forte Village Resort. This spa offers a variety of treatments using the healing powers of seawater and algae, including thalassotherapy, which involves soaking in heated seawater and receiving underwater massages.

Other popular spa resorts in Sardinia include the Chia Laguna Resort, which has a beautiful outdoor spa area overlooking the sea, and the Hotel Romazzino, which offers a range of traditional and modern treatments using local herbs and oils.

If you're looking for a more budget-friendly spa experience, there are also plenty of day spas and wellness centers throughout the island. These may not offer the same level of luxury as the resorts, but they can still provide a relaxing and rejuvenating experience.

When choosing a spa in Sardinia, it's important to consider the types of treatments and facilities available, as well as the location and cost. Many spas require advanced booking, especially during peak season, so be sure to plan ahead to avoid disappointment. Whether you're looking for a quick massage or a full day of pampering, a visit to a spa in Sardinia is sure to leave you feeling refreshed and rejuvenated.

## Attending a Traditional Festival

Sardinia is a region rich in tradition and culture, and one of the best ways to experience this is by attending one of the island's many traditional festivals. Sardinia has a long history of folk festivals that are celebrated throughout the year, with each one offering a unique insight into the island's customs and way of life.

One of the most popular festivals in Sardinia is the Carnival of Mamoiada, which takes place in February. This festival is known for its colorful masks and costumes, as well as the traditional dances and music that accompany the parade. Another popular festival is the Sagra del Redentore, which takes place in July and involves a procession of boats carrying a statue of Christ across the lagoon to the island of San Pietro.

The Sant'Efisio festival, which takes place in May, is one of the oldest and most important festivals in Sardinia. It commemorates the miraculous rescue of the island from the plague in 1652, and involves a procession of hundreds of people dressed in traditional costumes who walk from Cagliari to Nora, a distance of around 30 kilometers.

Other popular festivals in Sardinia include the Festival of Sant'Antonio Abate, which takes place in January and involves a parade of horses and riders, and the Festa di San Giovanni Battista, which takes place in June and involves the traditional sport of horse racing.

Attending a traditional festival in Sardinia is a unique and memorable experience, and a great way to immerse yourself in the island's culture and history. It's important to plan ahead, as some festivals may require advance booking for accommodation and transport. Be sure to check the festival schedule before planning your trip, and don't forget to bring your camera to capture the colorful and vibrant atmosphere of the festival.

# Tips for Creating Your Own Romantic Experiences

While Sardinia offers plenty of romantic experiences, there are also many ways to create your own unique and personalized romantic experiences on the island. Here are some tips for creating your own romantic moments in Sardinia:

**1. Choose a picturesque location:** Sardinia is full of beautiful beaches, hilltop towns, and scenic countryside that provide the perfect backdrop for a romantic moment. Whether it's a sunset picnic on the beach or a hike to a hilltop castle, choose a location that will make your partner feel special.

**2. Plan a surprise:** Surprising your partner with a thoughtful gesture can make any moment feel more romantic. Consider arranging a private boat tour, a hot air balloon ride, or a cooking class to add an element of surprise to your trip. You can also consider surprising your partner with a piece of local jewelry, a bottle of Sardinian wine, or a piece of art from a local artisan.

**3. Indulge in local cuisine:** Sardinia has a rich culinary tradition, and there's nothing more romantic than sharing a meal with your partner. Try some of the island's traditional dishes, such as fregola with clams, roast suckling pig, or seadas (a type of fried pastry filled with cheese and honey).

**4. Take a stroll:** Whether it's a leisurely walk through a historic town or a hike through the countryside, taking a stroll with your partner is a great way to create a romantic moment. Make sure to hold hands and take in the sights and sounds of your surroundings.

**5. Plan a spa day:** Sardinia is home to many luxurious spas that offer a range of treatments and services. Treat your partner to a massage, a soak in a thermal pool, or a relaxing steam bath to create a romantic and indulgent experience.

Remember, creating a romantic experience is all about the little details and showing your partner that you care.

# CHAPTER 5

## Essential Sardinian Travel Information

As your trip to Sardinia draws near, it's important to equip yourself with the essential travel information you need to make the most of your journey. This chapter will serve as a comprehensive guide to all the crucial information you need to know before you go. From Sardinia's currency and language to its emergency services and local customs, this chapter covers all the important details you need to ensure a smooth and stress-free trip. So sit back, relax, and get ready to dive into the practicalities of traveling in Sardinia.

## Sardinia's Weather and Climate

Sardinia's weather and climate is influenced by its location in the Mediterranean Sea, and it can vary greatly depending on the time of year you visit. Generally, Sardinia enjoys a mild Mediterranean climate with warm summers and mild winters.

Summer in Sardinia runs from June to September, and this is the peak tourist season when the island is busiest. During these months, the temperature can reach highs of around 30°C (86°F), and the sea temperature is warm enough for swimming. This is the perfect time to enjoy Sardinia's beautiful beaches, but it can also be quite hot and humid.

Spring and autumn are considered the shoulder seasons in Sardinia, and they are excellent times to visit if you want to avoid the crowds of summer. During these months, the weather is mild and comfortable, with temperatures ranging from around 15°C to 25°C (59°F to 77°F). It's also a good time for outdoor activities like hiking and exploring the island's natural beauty.

Winter in Sardinia can be chilly, especially in the mountainous regions of the island. The temperature can drop to around 10°C (50°F) or lower, and there can be rain and strong winds.

However, it's still possible to enjoy Sardinia in winter, especially if you're interested in cultural activities like visiting museums or historical sites.

It's important to note that Sardinia's weather can be unpredictable, so it's always a good idea to check the forecast before you go. In general, the island experiences a lot of sunshine throughout the year, so be sure to pack sunscreen and a hat to protect yourself from the sun's rays.

Overall, Sardinia's climate is mild and comfortable throughout most of the year, with peak tourist season in the summer months. Whether you prefer warm beach days or cooler outdoor adventures, there's always a perfect time to visit Sardinia.

## Health and Safety Information

When planning a trip to Sardinia, it is important to consider the health and safety aspects of your journey. Here are some essential tips and information to keep in mind:

**1. Vaccinations:** There are no required vaccinations for Sardinia. However, it is always a good idea to ensure you are up to date on routine vaccinations such as measles, mumps, rubella, and tetanus.

**2. Medical facilities:** Sardinia has a good standard of medical care, with several hospitals and clinics throughout the island. It is recommended to have travel insurance that covers medical emergencies and to bring any necessary medications with you.

**3. Emergency numbers:** In case of an emergency, the general emergency number in Italy is 112. For medical emergencies, you can also call 118.

**4. Crime:** Sardinia is a relatively safe destination, with low crime rates compared to other parts of Italy. However, it is still advisable to take precautions such as not leaving valuables unattended in public places and staying aware of your surroundings, particularly in tourist areas.

**5. Natural hazards:** Sardinia has a rugged and mountainous landscape, and visitors should be aware of potential hazards such as falling rocks, steep drops, and unstable ground. It is also important to take precautions against sunburn and heatstroke during the summer months.

**6. Local customs and laws:** Visitors to Sardinia should be aware of local customs and laws, particularly when it comes to driving and alcohol consumption. It is illegal to drive with a blood alcohol level over 0.5%, and penalties can be severe.

**7. Language:** The official language of Sardinia is Italian, although many locals also speak Sardinian. It is a good idea to learn some basic Italian phrases before your trip, particularly if you plan to visit smaller towns and villages where English may not be widely spoken.

By keeping these tips in mind, you can ensure a safe and healthy trip to Sardinia.

# Cultural Customs and Etiquette

As a traveler, it's important to respect and appreciate the local customs and traditions of the places you visit. This is especially true when it comes to Sardinia, as the island has a rich cultural heritage and unique customs that visitors should be aware of in order to avoid any unintentional cultural faux pas.

One of the most important things to keep in mind when traveling in Sardinia is the concept of "gallura" - a code of behavior that emphasizes respect, hospitality, and good manners. In general, Sardinians are very friendly and welcoming people, but it's important to remember to show respect for their culture and traditions.

Here are some other important cultural customs and etiquette to keep in mind when traveling in Sardinia:

**1. Dress conservatively:** Sardinia is a Catholic island, and as such, it's important to dress conservatively when visiting churches or other religious sites. It's also a good idea to dress modestly when walking around town, as Sardinians tend to dress formally and may be put off by overly casual or revealing clothing.

**2. Greet people properly:** When meeting someone for the first time, it's customary to greet them with a handshake and a smile. If you're meeting someone of the opposite sex, it's polite to wait for them to extend their hand first.

**3. Respect elders:** In Sardinian culture, elders are highly respected and revered. If you're introduced to an older person, it's customary to greet them with a kiss on both cheeks.

**4. Learn a few key phrases:** Although most Sardinians speak Italian, many also speak a local dialect called Sardo. Learning a few key phrases in Sardo or Italian can go a long way in showing respect for the local culture and making a good impression on locals.

**5 . Don't be too loud or boisterous:** Sardinians tend to be reserved and don't appreciate loud or boisterous behavior. It's important to be respectful of their quiet and peaceful way of life.

**6. Follow dining etiquette:** If you're invited to a Sardinian home for a meal, it's customary to bring a small gift such as a bottle of wine or a box of chocolates. When dining, it's important to wait for the host to start eating before you begin, and to keep your elbows off the table.

By following these cultural customs and etiquette, you'll be able to fully immerse yourself in Sardinian culture and make the most of your travels to this beautiful island.

## Useful Phrases in Sardinian

Sardinian, also known as Sardu, is a Romance language spoken on the Italian island of Sardinia. While Italian is the official language of the region, many locals still speak Sardinian, and visitors may find it useful to know some common phrases in the language.

*Here are some useful phrases in Sardinian:*

✓ **Bonu di (Morning) / Buona dì (Afternoon) / Bona serata (Evening) - Good morning / afternoon / evening**

✓ **Comente estes? - How are you?**

✓ **Beni, gràtzi - Fine, thank you**

✓ **De nada - You're welcome**

✓ **Ciao - Hello / Goodbye**

✓ **Adiu - Goodbye (more formal)**

✓ **Parlas sardu? - Do you speak Sardinian?**

✓ **Non parlo sardu - I don't speak Sardinian**

✓ **Mi chiamo [your name] - My name is [your name]**

✓ **Perdono - Excuse me**

✓ **Prego - Please**

✓ **Gràtzi - Thank you**

✓ **Quanto costa? - How much does it cost?**

✓ **Dove si trova...? - Where is...?**

✓ **Mi dispiatze - I'm sorry**

Learning a few phrases in the local language can go a long way in making a good impression and communicating effectively with the locals. It shows that you have taken an interest in their culture and are making an effort to connect with them.

## Money-Saving Tips For Your Trip

Sardinia, known for its natural beauty, rich history, and luxury accommodations, can be a costly destination. However, there are ways to save money without sacrificing your experience. Here are some tips for saving money on your trip to Sardinia:

**1. Travel during the off-season:** If you're flexible with your travel dates, consider visiting

Sardinia during the off-season (October to April), when hotel rates and airfares are generally lower. Additionally, during the off-season, you can still enjoy the mild climate, fewer crowds, and the island's natural beauty.

**2. Book in advance:** Book your accommodations, flights, and tours well in advance to get the best prices. Many hotels and tour operators offer early booking discounts, so plan your trip early to take advantage of these deals.

**3. Stay in budget-friendly accommodations:** Instead of staying in luxury resorts, consider staying in budget-friendly accommodations such as hostels, guesthouses, or vacation rentals. These accommodations can be significantly cheaper than luxury resorts while still providing comfortable accommodations.

**4. Use public transportation:** Sardinia's public transportation system is efficient and affordable. Consider using buses, trains, or ferries to get around the island instead of renting a car, which can be expensive.

**5. Eat like a local:** Sardinian cuisine is delicious and can be affordable if you eat like a local. Look for trattorias and pizzerias that serve authentic Sardinian dishes at reasonable prices.

**6. Avoid tourist traps:** Tourist traps can be expensive and often offer subpar experiences. Instead, seek out local experiences, such as visiting small towns, exploring hidden beaches, and attending traditional festivals.

**7. Shop smart:** Sardinia is known for its high-quality craftsmanship, but these items can be expensive. Shop at local markets and seek out artisans who sell their wares directly to customers to find unique souvenirs at reasonable prices.

By following these money-saving tips, you can have a fantastic trip to Sardinia without breaking the bank.

# CONCLUSION

After reading this travel guide, I hope that you feel excited and confident about planning your romantic getaway to Sardinia. With its stunning beaches, rich history, delicious cuisine, and warm hospitality, Sardinia offers an unforgettable experience for couples looking to escape and reconnect. Remember to take advantage of the many resources available to you, from tour operators and travel agencies to online reviews and social media groups. With a little research and preparation, your trip to Sardinia is sure to be a success!

## Final Tips for a Memorable Romantic Getaway to Sardinia

1. Be flexible and open to unexpected experiences.

2. Take time to slow down and savor each moment

3. Don't be afraid to ask locals for recommendations.

4. Be respectful of the island's natural beauty and cultural heritage.

5. And most importantly, enjoy each other's company and create lasting memories together.

# Resources for Further Travel Planning

✓ Sardinia Tourism Board website

✓ Tripadvisor's Sardinia forum

✓ Sardinia travel blogs and Instagram accounts

✓ Local tour operators and travel agencies

## Acknowledgements

I would like to express my gratitude to the Sardinia Tourism Board, as well as the local businesses and individuals who provided me with valuable insights and recommendations for this travel guide. I also want to thank my readers for choosing this guide and allowing me to share my passion for Sardinia with you. I hope that your trip to this magical island exceeds your expectations and leaves you with memories to treasure for a lifetime.

Have fun, *PHOENIX CARES!*

Made in the USA
Las Vegas, NV
16 December 2023

82975110R10046